HELPING OUR JAMAICAN BOYS ACHIEVE ACADEMIC SUCCESS:

A PARENT'S GUIDEBOOK FOR PROMOTING READING WITH BEGINNING READERS

By

Margaret Clarke B.Ed., M.Ed., Ed. D.
Jamaican Educator

With

Jim Paul, B.A., B.Ed., M.Ed. Ph.D.
Canadian Professor

Guide Introduction

"To read is to fly: it is to soar to a point of vantage which gives a view over wide terrains of history, human variety, ideas, shared experience and the fruits of many inquiries."
—A.C. Grayling

(From a *Financial Times* review of *A History of Reading* by Alberto Manguel. Accessed from: http://www.scribd.com/doc/18583266/Prof-aC-Grayling-In-a-Review-of-A-History-Of; January 2013)

HELPING OUR JAMAICAN BOYS
ACHIEVE ACADEMIC SUCCESS:
A PARENT'S GUIDEBOOK FOR PROMOTING
READING WITH BEGINNING READERS

Published by
WTL International
930 North Park Drive
P.O. Box 33049
Brampton, Ontario
L6S 6A7 Canada

www.wtlipublishing.com

ISBN 978-1-927865-26-2

Printed in the USA and Canada

10 9 8 7 6 5 4 3 2 1

Table of Contents

Introduction

"Have you asked yourself the question, "Why is reading important?" What was the answer that you got? I am sure your heart must have answered in favor of reading. Reading is like providing the mind with nourishment. Knowledge is the food for the mind and the soul. Apart from giving us the basic information about the world around us, it also provides us with the food for thought. It encourages us to think. It increases our hunger for knowledge and our thirst to learn more."
—A.C. Grayling

(From a *Financial Times* review of *A History of Reading* by Alberto Manguel. Accessed from: http://www.scribd.com/doc/18583266/Prof-aC-Grayling-In-a-Review-of-A-History-Of; January 2013)

The historical and contemporary unsatisfactory academic performance of male students in the Jamaican education system has been, is and must be of great concern to any society that seeks to improve its cultural, economic, and governance structures and infrastructures. Individual researchers in Jamaica have dedicated considerable attention and the Jamaican Ministry of Education has expended large sums of monies in numerous attempts to understand and address this crisis plaguing Jamaican male students, and yet the situation seems unchanged. This problem seems to extend beyond the borders of our home front and into communities abroad where Jamaican immigrants and second generation Jamaican immigrants have made their homes in places like the United States and Canada. Many boys descending from Jamaica are failing to read well and write properly. Certainly, not all our boys are under-performing academically, however, we, as a people are living in denial if we do not acknowledge the existence of a crisis that has and currently exists especially among our boys.

As an educator in Jamaica and as a researcher who dedicated my doctoral thesis to this topic, I (Dr. Margaret Clarke) truly believe that of those boys who are underperforming, the key common thread among them can be put in terms of literacy acquisition. Many of them have poor literacy. This guidebook is based on my doctoral studies research, completed in 2011, whereby I worked with several successful Jamaican male students who were performing very well academically. I went to these boys and asked them to share their literacy—reading and writing—achievements with me. I asked them directly: "How did you learn to read so well?" I asked these excellent young boys to design an effective, efficient and positive series of learning experiences for their peers that would invite them and enable them to become successful students. I think we all know that being a successful reader is a core ability and skill necessary for academic success. It is the specific literacy-centered advice offered by these young men that grounds this parent guidebook. These "best learning to read practices" were, therefore, identified by looking through the eyes of these young, successful boys. Parents and teachers should find this information beneficial in helping to change the learning landscape of Jamaica, on the island and wherever beyond its shores Jamaica's roots extend.

What follows is a simple guidebook focused on reading success for beginning and, perhaps, disenfranchised or reluctant young readers. This guidebook is the first of its kind—it is a guide aiming to advance academic achievement through the suggestions of literacy-successful boys. The suggestions provide insight into simple ways that literacy programmes can be brought alive effectively and efficiently. This is a must if more young boys are to be saved from the current literacy crisis evident within our community.

A word to the parents of young boys learning to read:
Did you know...?

First and foremost, parents, by virtue of being parents, are a child's *first* and, indeed, *most important* teachers. A child has the right to expect that his or her parents will teach him/her to become a good and productive citizen. A child learns by watching, interacting with, listening to and eventually talking with his or her parents. This relationship-learning process is at the heart and soul of a child becoming a successful lifelong reader.

A child learns through his or her life experiences, the modeling behaviors and actions he witnesses of his parents and his experiences of the ever-present expectations of the culture and society in which he lives and functions. All these elements are the learning and teaching contexts within which a child learns many life lessons including learning to read. As parents and as first teachers, we must accept that most of our children really want to learn to read and they expect to learn to read. They have the right to learn; we have that responsibility to teach.

Learning to read happens when a child:
- Sees himself/herself as successful before s/he is capable, AND a parent believes and lives as if a child will be a good reader;
- Is able to maintain confidence through the learning to read process, AND s/he is actively supported by a parent's love and care;
- Is given time and opportunity to support what is being taught at school regarding reading; AND a parent both provides and protects a home learning and teaching time and space; and,
- Has parents who understand that reading well is the result of guided practice, AND a parent is that guide; and,
- Spends time with his parents learning to read, AND the process is both fun and challenging.

Parental Notes:

Why is this guide needed?

"The more that you read, the more things you will know.
The more that you learn, the more places you'll go."
— Dr. Seuss, *I Can Read With My Eyes Shut!*

In Jamaica, like most countries around the world, the ability to achieve educational academic success does not begin at school with our teachers, but rather the foundations for schooling success begins at home with our nation's parents. This view of academic success is supported by a sample of post-elementary Jamaican male students who participated in a recent doctoral research study (Clarke, 2011). A significant theme that was evident in that research study which focused on student academic success and literacy—reading and writing—had every study participant agreeing that their journey to academic success and schooling achievements began at home with the support of and teachings of their parents, or grandparents, or caregivers. In fact, these young Jamaican boys, in my doctoral research study believed, emphatically, that learning to read and write, and to do so well with effectiveness, must begin as a family affair and the important literacy processes of learning to read and to appreciate reading must begin and be reinforced at home.

However, let us remind ourselves, as parents and as first-teachers, what academic success really is. As well, we must realize why academic success and achievement are so important for learners themselves, their parents, our educators, and this nation. So, I ask this question: "What are the characteristics of an academically successful student?" Obviously, responses to that question have evolved over the years as schools have changed and as curriculum and instruction have evolved and the nation itself and socioeconomics and politics have changed. That is, what it meant to be successful, as a parent or a teacher when either was in school is probably not necessarily the achievement standard that today's students are being assessed on and judged by. Although the definition of being a "successful academic student" has changed over the years and across generations, contemporary school children still must hold, and be able to use well, the basic learning, knowing and doing building blocks of literacy and numeracy. Again, that means today's students must have skills with attributes that foster reading, writing, and arithmetic. To be a successful learner and citizen in the early 21st century a student must demonstrate:

- Abilities to analyze, synthesize, and evaluate information and knowledge;
- Abilities to effectively communicate with others using appropriate intent and form;

- Proficiency in job, career and professional foundational subjects such as: the sciences (biology, chemistry, physics), mathematics, computer/technical skills, foreign languages, as well as history, geography, and global awareness;
- Capabilities of collaboratively working in culturally diverse settings;
- Leadership by designing, initiating and seeing projects with others through to completion;
- Responsible decision-making, and being self-motivated and active as political citizens; and
- Ethically committed to their families, communities, colleagues and nation (Nidds & McGerald, 1996).

Simply, none of these "success" characteristics above would even be available to most learners unless they were taught to appreciate how to learn at home, and this appreciation was then acknowledged and utilized early in their schooling. There is evidence to suggest that limited success academically awaits many students who have not been empowered with the appreciation for reading—and that does not mean that every young boy learns to read well at home before school; rather that he has an appreciation for reading and he is willing to try to learn to read well.

This guide, then, is dedicated to sharing rigorous research conducted in our Jamaican context with a team of young boys who have been and are very successful by today's school measures of academic success. And, why are these Jamaican young boys successful? Again, simply, they became effective and efficient learners at school and in their communities, first and foremost, with the literacy guidance of their parents and, second, their school teachers in their early schooling years built on their initial engagements with reading as provided by their parents, or grandparents or caregivers.

There were many negative issues the boys in the research project pointed to in terms of why they felt a literacy crisis exists among many of their male peers. However, these issues have been well documented in Jamaica by the government or the media or by its concerned citizens and they range from a lack of positive citizen male role models, to the seduction reward attraction of crime, or high unemployment, and so on. However, the purpose of this guide is not to go in that direction of speculating about literacy crisis causes or problems or poverties, but rather to attend to the voices of wise boys who have been successful academically.

The boys in my research study felt, in a show of wisdom, that there is too much negativity regarding Jamaican boys and the youth literacy crisis. As a Jamaican mother, professional teacher, and literacy researcher, I agreed. Most research studies conducted in Jamaica regarding the male learner literacy crisis repeatedly focus on the poverty-stricken nature of the cause and the observable impacts of the crisis. My research study boys remind us that it is our responsibility as Jamaicans to become locally and nationally engaged in discussions about what must count, be designed as, and realized as a positive literacy learning process for all learners—

6

and especially young male learners many of whom who are at risk. As such, my research study boys have identified vital literacy skills such as phonics, sight vocabulary, vocabulary enrichment, structural analysis, and comprehension skills as being crucial to their learning and academic success. Obviously, these are school-learned attributes and skills. However, the boys agreed that these literacy skills that make them academically successful in school are deeply linked to how their parents, or grandparents, or caregivers invited them to begin to become first readers. It is to share these successful boys' insights that give this guide its importance and practicality.

Our reading aloud to our boys causes their brains to become conditioned to associating pleasure, meaning, curiosity and problem solving with reading. Reading aloud—adult to child and child to adult—serves to establish in the boy a comprehension and knowledge and experience background to which other information and experiences may be added and from which information can be drawn to make sense of new and varied knowledge and experiences. These are the essential qualities of the learning process—and if your child has experienced these processes he should flourish with school teachers. Therefore, the vocabulary of our boys (first as listeners, then as speakers) grows larger as does their ability to comprehend and use language and, we, the readers as parents, become a model for them.

Our parental goal, however, in terms of literacy remains simple—we read to our boys so they go beyond our reading to them and they can successfully read texts, people, and the world by themselves. So, reading aloud to our children is really the beginning of the more formal learning and teaching reading processes. Reading, and in particular reading aloud, to young boys lays the foundation for their future success in learning to read personally, pragmatically and academically.

Jamaica's 2030 vision is to ensure that we, as a people, achieve the equivalent of first world status. This objective, though laudable, will only be attainable when all members of our society today and tomorrow, particularly young males, have attained the literacy skills necessary to live strong, balanced and functional lives. To ensure our nationhood as an independent and yet globally participating people, we, as Jamaicans, must understand that being an educated people is our first and foremost task. The globalizing situation that now exists in Jamaica demands that all learners, male and female, young and mature, wealthy and poor be adept at mastering the foundational skills of literacy—especially relating to reading—in order for all Jamaicans to be productive local, national and international citizens. The power is in our hands and I believe it lies within the attainable literacy-promoting practices and recommendations that follow.

Parental Notes:

Introducing the appreciation of reading to a child as a parent, grandparent or caregiver

"Children are made readers on the laps of their parents."
—Emilie Buchwald

There are a number of pointers you'll want to remember and put into practice as you introduce the appreciation of reading to your child. There will also be some typical observations that you can expect as you implement reading. In this section, you'll explore these pointers and will encounter brief segments on some of these observations you can expect that are normal—even good signposts. Please note, from this point and beyond, the word "parent" may be used interchangeably with the words "grandparent" and "caregiver" and the word "son" may be adjusted accordingly.

Make a Reading Impression

Each research study participant in my study recalled his mother, brother, sister, aunt, cousin or grandparent playing a very active role in assisting him with his early learning-to-read experiences and the initial establishing of his early reading skills. In this regard, let us read one of the participants' responses. Juicy said:

> Miss, my mother, grandmother and aunt helped me to learn to read. They would tell me stories, and then ask me questions about the story. They would also ask me to spell words for them. I had fun listening to the stories being told to me especially the Anancy[1] stories. Anancy is cunning, smart and always able to escape trouble no matter the situation. (Participant Interview, September 30, 2008)

---

[1] The Ashanti handed down to the Jamaican peoples a series of brilliant folktales about the trickster Anancy, the spider-man. Many of these folktales are accompanied by songs and/or have inspired many Jamaican folksongs.

A child's first experiences with literacy (especially reading and, of course, writing) depends on the ways in which parents and/or other caregivers actually use themselves, and demonstrate reading and writing in their own personal and working lives. Children who live in a home environment where reading and writing are used and displayed as skills to achieve or fulfill daily needs will gradually learn to appreciate the value of such skills. Children mimic—for better or worse—those behaviors and actions and words they witness and experience. In other words, since children live what they learn and learn what they live, it is best to immerse them in the activities or behaviors that we, as parents or caregivers, want them to actually practice. Reading and writing are extremely important skills in the contemporary world that parents should be modeling. And this modeling is simple to do, if and only if, a parent or caregiver remains committed to doing so. Remember, children are impressionable—so we must make a reading impression; the results in the long-run are remarkable for a child, and the return to the parent or caregiver is immeasurable. Imagine your young reader sitting and turning pages and telling you that he is reading and he is enjoying doing so!

Read Aloud

A significant and, perhaps, foundational aspect of the literacy research with this group of academically successful young boys, was the powerful impact that a parent or caregiver had on them when he or she read aloud to the boys.

Let us examine some of the benefits of the simple parental act of reading aloud to our boys. Trelease (2001) states that when we read to our child we re-assure, entertain, bond with, inform and inspire him or her, and we teach him, or her, to know, become and do. In the very simple act of reading aloud to our boys we, as parents, also condition their brains to associate reading with the pleasure of belonging; and, we create, as well, attributes and abilities regarding background knowledge, and we build vocabulary, enhance comprehension and provide a reading role model for our boys. Such a simple act as taking the time to read to a boy aloud provides multiple returns for the child, and it feels good for the parent as well. It is a true gift to our boys offered by their parents, to read aloud to them.

It is very important, in establishing a learning attitude regarding reading early with boys, that we re-assure our boys by reading for, to, or with him. By doing this form of oral reading engagement, each parent is removing the dread or fear associated with learning to read which some boys have. As often as a parent reads a story to boys aloud—and boys, we know, often take longer developmentally to mature in terms of the acquisition of literacy skills—the more readily that a boy commits a story, song, poem, or narrative and associated words and images to memory. Shortly after several readings, the child will be seen and heard re-telling the story or narrative on his own. The stories will become a source of play and imagination and a way of meaning-making, problem solving, and transference for the boy—all of which foundationally will come into play later in the boy's school learning. When he begins to write, it will be the words learned from the stories or songs or poems that he will use to construct his own stories, poems, or songs. As the process is repeated, the inherent ability to read increases—indeed, confidence in being able to lift alphabetic symbols from the page and to use those symbols as language based on memorized content also increases. Imagine your young child greeting you with a story that he wrote for you based on his favourite stories that you have been reading aloud for him. Parental excitement should abound.

The More Time Invested the Better

In addition, actual literacy research has shown that one predictor of a child's literacy achievement in terms of reading and writing, and in terms of academic success in school, is the number of contact hours he was read to as a preschooler (Wells in McGee & Richgells, 2008). Simply put the literacy activities that parents or caregivers engage in do actually serve to motivate boys to become interested in these activities. Children enjoy nothing more than spending time and sharing a space with their parents; it is a sign of love, attention and caring. Parents, therefore, need to become aware that they are their child's first real teachers. Parents fill that role whether they wish to accept that role or not. The language experiences that parents or caregivers provide during the literacy activities done at home will have powerful effects on the boy's later growth in literacy. This is a proven fact. Some children can overcome a poverty-stricken literacy, but it requires a special kind of child, a special kind of opportunity later in life, and a special kind of person who actually spends time teaching like the parent that child needed in the first place. Imagine your young child making a presentation to his class using correctly, the language that you modeled for him through your read aloud sessions.

Motivate Them

The research study boys felt that both at home and especially at school, the Jamaican male literacy crisis may have been deepened in terms of the lack of readiness of boys to accept the right and responsibility to read well when they enter school. Why? Simply, often the boys' parents or caregivers had not taken the time to motivate the boys to appreciate learning to read well. Parents worked hard to provide shelter, clothing and food for the boys, but often they simply didn't make time to foster an appreciation of learning to read with their boys. The research study boys felt that even a simple act such as inviting young boys to contribute to and participate in the selection of texts would be a most basic but reading-appreciation-building activity with their parents or caregivers. If boys are not invited to be motivated to read, then they often struggle later with reading. Motivation to learn and the ability to learn are interconnected. The boys in the study felt that a major improvement—both at home and during their early and late schooling years—was in the direction to attention to their role as active agents in their own learning. Again, simply, the boys indicated that when they are given a choice of what to have

11

read to them or to read themselves, they are choosing to do something—to learn. Remember the choice is between reading this or that or not reading at all. Imagine your son asking you to take him to the bookshop or the library to select a book that he would love to read. Your heart should swell with joy. Imagine him reading a Hardy Boys book or a Nancy Drew in a week because it was his choice. Or it could be two comics. He reads and enjoys reading them. Wow!

What to Expect: It May Test Your Patience

Have patience with the evolving boy but do not stop being a good reading teacher. Know that successful acquisition of reading as an attribute, ability and skill in a child is demonstrated through his questioning mind that seeks answers to the questions about self, other and life.

Be Expressive

As we as parents or caregivers, read the stories to the best of our own reading abilities with enthusiasm, and as we use our voices to represent the characters in the story, or add expression to the mood or atmosphere, or we use our voices to make sound effects, we entertain our children with the joy of reading. Such an engagement is pleasurable—even if the life outside the home is not. The modulation of our voices, the expressions on our faces and the gesticulations that we make with our hands all serve to entertain our children who will often ask for many re-readings of each story. Combining actions with each story really works. Embodied reading is pleasurable. Boys learn through their bodies and kinesthetic learning, linked to literacy learning, enables boys to accelerate their learning. Each re-reading helps to re-enforce a model of good and pleasurable reading. Imagine your boys going to school with a hands-on reading attitude.

What to Expect: He Will Want to Read As Time Passes

Importantly, when we, as parents or caregivers, read aloud to our children, a bond is being formed between the children and ourselves and the texts we read. We are showing and telling reading engagement and through these guided practices, the child will soon seek reader independence—and why? Simply, he will want to show and tell their parents or caregivers that he can read—and read well! Soon each adult reader and child listener comes to exchange roles. The reader, who is initially the parent, soon realizes that in reading aloud to his or her boy listener a literacy bond is formed and eventually, in the time together, the boy proudly reads to his parent or caregiver. The boy recognizes that the reader, his parent, is enabling him to enjoy an activity that he is not yet able to do by himself—read a text. So, he strives to show that he can. Imagine a boy heading to school who wants to show adults what he can do.

Explain or Look Up the Unfamiliar

As we read to our children, it is important that we explain unfamiliar words or ideas to them. Overlooking unfamiliar words and ideas because you, the parent, believe that your son will not understand the term or concept fully serves only to rob him of a richer and fuller understanding of the story in that moment. As well, as the child matures to greater levels of understanding of a text, if a word or concept eludes him, then his understanding of the text is lessened because of this. Additionally, by not addressing unknown words or concepts, the child is being taught to skip over difficulties instead of trying to work through them. If you, as a parent, are uncertain of a word or concept in the text, then there is a pedagogic opportunity to show the child how to solve the issue of not knowing. A parent doesn't need to know everything. Being honest is important when being honest includes—"I don't know son, but I will try to find out." And, when you say this, it actually means you have to "find out." That teaching makes a remarkable impact on our boys as they witness a parent who finds things out that s/he does not know. Imagine a boy going to school with the ability to find things out for himself and who is a trust-worthy problem-solver.

What to Expect: Curiosity

Curiosity and inspiration are aroused as we read aloud to our boys. When we read aloud to them and they begin to ask questions, we need to realize that they have become more curious and that they want to understand more. The length and complexity of the texts should increase. They are inspired to seek to know more—you did that as a parent. This awakened desire should not be deferred, or ignored, or attacked, but instead should be nurtured by our truthfully answering their questions and curiosities.

Parental Notes:

Ten easy steps to follow for reading aloud with your son effectively

How does one—a parent—engage in reading aloud? This is a great question and what follows are some specific suggestions. These suggestions focus on boys—our sons—who often need a concentrated, attentive approach to being read to. So, some suggestions the boys made were:

1

Allow your son to help select—to negotiate a topic is an important conversational ability and asset—the text and topic he wants you to read for or with him. The text selected makes a difference. A text is a good text if it stimulates interesting talk between a parent and a child. Loving just one good text may establish a life-long reader. An added benefit is that by talking about what to read you also get to know your son better. That may mean that you have to have texts available to choose from that have colorful or interesting images on the front cover, or interesting titles, or your brief response to "What is the text about?" is engaging.

If you are wondering what you might read aloud to your pre-school son(s), here is a brief listing of easily accessible and useful books for example:

- *The Little Red Hen*
- *Click, Clack, Moo, Cows that Type*
- *Chicken Little*
- *The Little Engine that Could*
- *Mrs. Wishy Washy*
- *The Three Little Pigs*
- *The True Story of the Three Little Pigs*
- *The Big Bad Pig and the Three Little Wolves*

2

Select a quiet place and a regular time, if possible, to do the reading so it is an enjoyable and predictable event. Children enjoy stability and routine. They enjoy looking forward toward something happening. So setting a time for reading ensures that this activity will be done. A quiet place ensures "aloneness" with the person. It suggests "uninterruptedness" which guarantees quality. Reading at specific times and in a place free from distractions: a place where a child and a parent bond and share ideas forms a cord that will remain unbroken—a line that will become a generational blessing.

3

Ask questions to build interest in the text. Read the title of the text, try to name the key "good" character (protagonist) and the "difficult" or "bad" character (antagonist) and the names of the author and illustrator (if there is one). You do this because after several readings of a text or after reading several different texts, you invite your son to select his favorite text—but he must ask for it by name, or by author, or by topic, or by image, and so on.

Discuss the images (if they are present) on the cover or inside of the book. You do this because you want to work with your son on colors and differences in and between shapes and sizes, and what is fore-grounded and back-grounded in an image. Ask your son what he thinks happened just before the picture was frozen on the page (this is a recovery task) and what might happen next (this is an anticipation task). These processes introduce the concepts of perspective and tenses (past, present, and future) to the child.

Try to establish, prior to reading the text, the context of the text—that is: Focus on the child's prior experiences and/or knowledge about the text's subject or topic. Build up the child's motivation or desire for the text. This process of establishing a context for a text's subject matter or topic may be accomplished through a parent and a child:
- Recalling prior experiences and observations;
- Brainstorming or thinking imaginatively ;
- Texting about the subject or topic talk;
- Engaging in a question and answer session;
- Drawing pictures or painting about the text's subject or topic;
- Listening to music or songs regarding the text's subject or topic;
- Looking at pictures regarding the text's subject or topic;
- Creating predictions regarding the text's subject or topic;
- Role playing regarding the text's subject or topic.

4

Allow your son to tell you what he thinks the text or story will be about based on the title or cover page. You do this because you want to begin transferring the boy from being a passive to an engaged reader to eventually being an author or writer himself.

5

Read aloud and remember, your voice is the key to the reading experience for young boys—your voice must be heard and the variations in your voice must be heard, and felt, by your son. This reading voice is a private thing between you and your boy. Relax and have fun together as you are brought together by a book.

6

Read and pause to explain unfamiliar words or ideas to him. You do this because meaning is alive in the understanding of the details of a text and if a word is unfamiliar to your son then meaning is lost unless you help him understand; also, increasing comprehension depends on a larger and growing vocabulary. Perhaps, consult a dictionary, an encyclopedia, a librarian, a knowing friend, a co-worker or colleague, or use the Internet.

The parents who are aware of their literacy responsibilities will further encourage their child's literacy development by enabling him to make the connections between the words committed to memory and the words written in the story. This can be done by simply highlighting these words, or through the use of word cards, or using songs or playing word games such as "I Spy with My Little Eye" or "The Postman."

7

Go over sections of the story that agree or disagree with his predictions. Ask him what the next page may reveal. You do this because you want to begin to invite your sons to become analytical critical readers. He will begin to engage in reasoned and rational cases for or against something and cite evidence to make his case.

8

Focus on the child's understandings of the intention of the text through questions and prompting statements. Ask, does the text tell a story? Explain, describe, make a case for or against, and so on. Focus on the child's understandings of the author's intent—what does the author intend for his audience to experience—and the text's content and structure or form. For example, a book that intends to explain to a person how to fix a motorbike is a different kind of writing than a book that tells a story. Focus on the child's ability to deal with the text's difficulty. This process of focusing on the reading task may be accomplished through:

- On first reading, just skimming or quickly reading the text for some highlights of the information presented;
- Then, talking about organizational features of the text, or making more predictions about the text or asking the questions about the text—that is, both child and adult may ask questions of each other;
- And then a slower, more careful re-reading of the text.

Try to comprehend the text's meaning. Focus on the child's experiencing of the text in a variety of ways—depending on the child's readiness and stage of reading development—such as independent reading by the child, guided reading whereby the parent helps the child to read, or the parent reads and the child listens. Focus on the child's understanding by going back over the text and his predictions made earlier about the text. Encourage the child to make his own comments about the text—its content, form, style, and so on.

Try to respond and consolidate meaning. Focus on reflecting on the text—focus on what the child felt and/or thought about the text. Focus on asking the child to respond to the text personally and critically. Focus on the child shaping and reshaping ideas about the text. Focus on asking the child to suggest creative ways to change the text. This process of responding and consolidating meaning may be achieved through:

- Sharing interpretations;
- Re-reading favourite parts of the text;
- Re-telling the story or parts of it; or
- Writing or drawing about the text.

As teaching parents, we must always build bridges between the text (a book, television show, film, website, picture or image, or song and so on) and the child's growing literacy experiences. When selecting texts to share, parents and children must select texts with care.

There are some simple reading comprehension suggestions for parents. With boys, always begin with concrete questions—for example: What is the name of the central character? Begin with what is evident in the text, so that you can actually point to it in the text, before going to more abstract questions—for example: What do you think the character's motivation was for acting as he did? Remember, a boy's brain hunts for information and based on that information, he acts, often quickly. If you ask him simple and direct questions initially, he will normally get them correct. This increases his confidence, and then a parent has something to build on—information. Try not to begin with questions such as WHY...? So, try to begin with more specific questions than general questions. Boys are generally not very good at going directly to expressing feelings or deep understandings about what they have read, so where possible, follow this simple line of direction when questioning boys about what they have read. It is this:

- Ask questions about what is exactly stated IN THE LINES of the text;
- Then ask questions about what is BETWEEN THE LINES of the text; and
- Then ask questions that are BEYOND THE LINES of the text.

Back in 1956, Benjamin Bloom identified six levels of intellectual behavior that are important to learning. He believed that learners must be asked questions from each level of his taxonomy or pyramid progressively with the level of "knowledge" as the base (or foundational) level and "evaluation" as the highest level of intellectual behavior. To help you as parent to assist your boy to understand or comprehend what he has learned, Bloom's Taxonomy with examples of questions or learning statements for a text about Usain Bolt is:

Level and Bloom's Term	Descriptor of Term	Example of questions or learning statements	Parent Space for notes
Level 6 **Evaluation** (Highest Level)	The judgment of characters, actions, and outcomes for personal reflection and understanding. This level includes recognizing subjectivity, verifying the value of evidence, and making choices based upon reason. To ask for this kind of information use words like: *grade, convince, support, recommend, measure,* and *conclude*.	Assess the strengths and weaknesses of the Olympics and recommend changes. Form a panel to discuss views on an important issue such as the Jamaican male literacy crisis.	
Level 5 **Synthesis**	The creative level whereby one uses old ideas to create new ones. This level consists of generalizing from given facts, relating knowledge from several areas, and drawing conclusions. To ask for this kind of information use words like: *combine, integrate, substitute, create, invent,* and *compose*.	When does sport become a business? Compose a song to celebrate Bolt's amazing legacy in athletics.	

Level 4 **Analysis** 	The comparison of the content to your own personal experiences. This level includes seeing patterns, identifying components, and recognizing hidden meanings. To ask for information use words like: *analyze, separate, order, classify, divide,* and *explain*.	How did you react to what Bolt did at the London 2016 Olympics? Contrast Jamaican Olympic athletes of today with those of the past.	
Level 3 **Application** 	The use of information, methods, concepts, and theories in new situations. To ask for this kind of information use words like: *apply, demonstrate, illustrate, solve, modify,* and *change*.	Modify an Olympic sport not yet open to the disabled athlete so it is a Paralympic sport for 2020. Illustrate what the entry uniforms should look like for the Jamaican team.	
Level 2 **Comprehension** 	This is an understanding of what was read. This level includes interpreting facts, comparing and contrasting, and predicting consequences. To ask for this kind of information use words like: *summarize, estimate, discuss, predict, interpret,* and *associate*.	Predict if Bolt will be able to compete in the 2020 Olympics? How does the quality of a coach and training partners affect an athlete, such as Bolt, in preparing for competition? Write a summary report of Bolt's 2016 Olympic events.	
Knowledge Level 1 (Base or Foundation Level) 	Straight recall of specific information in the text whether it be dates, events, places, ideas, or any subject matter. To ask for this kind of information use words like: *list, define, tell, describe, who, what,* and *where*.	Who is Usain Bolt? Define the Olympic Motto? Make a list of Bolt's Olympic winning times?	

(Adapted from material accessed via
http://www.coun.uvic.ca/learn/program/hndouts/bloom.html; January 2013)

9

Invite your son to extend or change the story or text. You do this because you want to activate the curiosity and wonderment elements in his brain. You want to stimulate the "what if," imaginative faculties of his brain.

Try to extend the text. Prompt your son to investigate how the information in the text applies to other scenarios? Or how he would add upon or alter the text? Focus on extending language experiences. This process of extending the text may be achieved through:

- Talking;
- Reading related texts;
- Writing in a variety of forms about the text;
- Researching different aspects of the text;

10

At the end of the story, allow your son to select an activity that he would love to do. For example, he can draw his favorite character, conjure up a different ending for the story, tell a similar but different story, make models of the characters in the story, create some simple puppets, play out the story, role-play, or play matching games, and so on.

Parental Notes:

Conclusion

Reading to your boy is the one thing—intellectually, emotionally, socially and physically—that feeds his growing and inquiring, literacy-obsessed brain. Every parent tries to work hard and long to make his/her boy's life better. In doing so you provide the safest place to live that you can and the best food you can to eat. You teach him how to play fairly, treat people respectfully, and be a good boy. What about teaching him to be a good reader and writer? Perhaps it is these two things that will enable him to be a good man, a strong father, a valuable employee/employer, and a contributing citizen. That pathway to successful reading and writing begins at home—just like most pathways for a boy—and, in this case, with the simple act of taking the time to read aloud to your boy. So, remember, in the beginning keep reading simple by keeping the activity itself simple, enjoyable and regular. In this process, you, as first-teacher, must present to your boy, the understanding that the reading process, simply, is a life-giving meaning-making process. We urge you to follow the steps suggested here so that we can close this gap among our boys through your vital role as parent, grandparent or caregiver.

References

Geisel, T.S. (Dr.Seuss) (1978). I can read with my eyes shut: A beginner's book. Random House International

Manguel, A. (2013). *Financial Times* review of *A History of Reading*. Accessed from: http://www.scribd.com/doc/18583266/Prof-aC-Grayling-In-a-Review-of-A-History-Of; January 2013]

McGee, L. & Richgells, D.(2008).Literacy's beginnings: Supporting young readers and writers. Boston: Allyn and Bacon

Nidds, J.A., & McGerald, J. (1996). Corporate America looks critically at public education: How should we respond? [Electronic version]. Contemporary Education, 67, 62-64.

Trelease, J. (1979). The read-aloud handbook. 5th Ed. New York: Penguin Publishers